UoLearn™
Easy 4 me 2 learn

Bestselling books by Heather Baker

Speed Writing, ISBN 978-1-84937-011-0

Successful Business Writing, ISBN 978-1-84937-074-5

Order books from your favorite bookseller or direct from www.uolearn.com

Successful minute taking – meeting the challenge.

How to prepare, write and organize agendas and minutes of meetings. Learn to take notes and write minutes of meetings. Your role as the minute taker and how you interact with the chair and other attendees.

Improve your writing skills. A Skills Training Course.
Lots of exercises and free downloadable workbook.

Published by: Universe of Learning Ltd, reg number 6485477, Lancashire, UK
www.UoLearn.com, support@UoLearn.com

ISBN 978-1-84937-076-9

Other editions: UK spelling version 978-1-84937-038-7
ebook pdf format 978-1-84937-040-0

Other imprints:
Easy 4 Me 2 Learn Writing minutes and Agendas and Taking notes at Meetings
978-1-84937-039-4

Skills Training Course, Universe of Learning and UoLearn are trademarks of Universe of Learning Ltd.

BakerWrite is a trademark of Baker Thompson Associates Ltd and is used with permission.

Photographs © www.fotolia.com
Edited by Dr Margaret Greenhall.

Dedication

This book is dedicated to all the wonderful people who have supported and inspired me over the years – my mother, Jean Thompson, my late father, John Thompson, the good school teachers and college lecturers (particularly Miss Lowcock, Mrs Pagliacci, Mrs Shelley and Angela Murphy), those managers and colleagues at ICI Pharmaceuticals, Cognac Hine, Hewlett Packard and ITV Granada who had faith in my abilities and gave me the confidence to progress and not forgetting all my friends along the way.

I would also like to thank the many, many people who have supported Baker Thompson Associates Limited since January 2000, including, of course, Margaret Greenhall, my publisher.

And, above all, my lovely family – Ian, Ailsa and Erin.

About the author: Heather Baker

Heather had over twenty years' experience as a secretary and PA before setting up Baker Thompson Associates Limited in 2000. The company specializes in the training and development of secretarial and administrative staff (www.bakerthompsonassoc. co.uk). She now travels all over the UK working with large and small companies to enable their office staff and PAs to work more effectively and efficiently. She also delivers courses in the Middle and Far East. Heather is a Certified NLP Practitioner.

She worked for ICI Pharmaceuticals (now AstraZeneca) and Hewlett Packard; she spent 5 years in France working for the Commercial Director of Cognac Hine and then 10 years with Granada Media working up to personal assistant to the managing director, commuting regularly between their offices in Manchester and London.

Heather conceived the speed writing system BakerWrite and wrote a bestselling book based on this system (Speed Writing Skills Training Course, www.UoLearn.com). The speed writing course is also available as an online learning course (www.bakerwrite.com). Her newest book is Successful Business Writing (www.UoLearn.com).

She has been married to Ian since 1979 and they have two daughters, Ailsa and Erin.

Praise for minute training

- ✓ "This is a superb book. I wish it had read it before I started organizing meetings, writing agendas and taking minutes years ago! It is full of really good tips and is very clear and easy to read. This will really help with coaching and mentoring junior members of staff."

- ✓ "I read it from cover to cover on the train on the way back from London today. I thought it was excellent and, for the first time (ever!), makes minute taking seem easy! So many books make you switch off! I particularly liked the tips and hints as you went along. I have the copy at work and when I have my next PA team meeting, I'm going to ask them all to borrow it and read it!"

- ✓ "As I always struggle taking minutes and it is an important part of my job I was looking for a book to help me to improve this skill. I have found this book to be invaluable especially the checklist at the back. I now feel happier taking minutes and as this used to be a job I dreaded, I feel this book is a must for anyone else in the same situation as me."

- ✓ "I had a real phobia about minute taking and was dreading today, but you've really taken away my fear. It's all fallen into place." Beverley, Leeds

- ✓ "This was a genuine workshop that taught skills and you came away knowing more than when you went in. Heather was keen to assess our expertise and worked with the group accordingly. Good to see someone presenting without constant reference to notes."

✓ "One of the best facilitators ever - quite clearly Heather had an extensive knowledge of the skills needed and she wanted to share best practice. She was keen to hear of other experiences, mixed the group up well and interacted with everyone."

✓ "This was an excellent workshop which clearly met all of its objectives. The course was well planned and the subject matter presented in a clear, logical and interesting way."

✓ "Heather had very good subject knowledge and is a very good trainer. She used a number of different teaching methods and was excellent at putting the group at ease; everyone joined in." Committee servicing and minute taking for Leeds Metropolitan University

✓ "The School has seen a vast improvement in minute taking since staff attended Heather Baker's minute taking session. This has been crucial for the forthcoming audits and we are very grateful to Heather. Staff have commented that instructions and presentation were good and it was a fun session with lots of useful material." Sheila Furmedge, ASIS and Staff Development Manager, University of Huddersfield

✓ "It was a really clear, structured course. Good pace (kept to the agenda!). Good to leave a course and feel like I can truly apply what I've learned to my role."
Minute taking for the National Audit Office

✓ "I'm fairly comfortable with taking minutes, but find I write a lot of notes in the meeting which probably aren't necessary. I've learned how to condense effectively."

✓ "Heather was very practical and helpful; understood the reality of taking minutes and not just the theory!"
Minute taking for RiverStone Management Limited

✓ "I enjoyed the course and found it relevant to my needs. The trainer was helpful and able to answer questions. She obviously enjoys her work and conveys her enthusiasm to delegates."

✓ "I found the course really useful and the style and delivery were very easy to understand."
Bespoke minute taking for Yorkshire Television

Agenda

Introduction

I'd rather throw myself downstairs....

That was how I used to feel about minute taking; this book is aimed at those among you who feel the same.

In 'the old days' secretarial courses didn't always include minutes as people did shorthand; however, minute taking is not just about taking notes, there is so much more to it.

Minute takers are often unprepared to do the job because they haven't learned what to do. Also, they are frequently asked to take notes just before a meeting starts or on the first day in a new job. This just won't work.

This book is aimed at secretaries, PAs and administrators and covers the issues that worry them. These are based on the things that worried me and the things that have worried my hundreds of delegates over the last 10 years.

The book has many exercises for you to develop your skills. There is space to write in the book but if you would prefer, you can download a printable copy of the exercises for you to write on from www.UoLearn.com. Some of the exercises have suggested answers and these can be found at the end of the book. If you have any questions you're welcome to email us at support@UoLearn.com.

Item 1:
Meetings

"When you go to meetings or auditions and
you fail to prepare, prepare to fail. It is simple but true."
Paula Abdul

Item 1: Meetings

Objectives for item 1, at the end of this item you will:

✓ Be aware of different types of meetings

✓ Understand the purposes and benefits of meetings

✓ Be able to outline why we have minutes

✓ Know the key elements of a successful meeting

✓ Have a list of business meeting terms and their definitions

✓ Have considered meetings within your organization

What types of meetings are there?

> **Annual General Meeting (AGM)**

A meeting held every year to inform an organization's members of previous and future activities. This meeting is often required by law or the constitution or charter of an organization. Directors and auditors may be appointed.

> **Extraordinary General Meeting**

As above, but set up for a specific, usually very important, reason.

> **Board meetings**

A management meeting involving the board of directors of an organization.

> **Committee meetings**

A meeting of a group set up from a larger group to manage specific issues.

> **Senior management meetings**

A meeting of senior members of an organization, but not including the board of directors.

> **Departmental meetings**

A meeting of the staff in a department for planning, discussion and reporting.

> **Staff meetings**

A meeting of all the staff from part of an organization.

> **Middle management meetings**

A meeting of staff who don't take part in board or senior management meetings and usually these meetings don't include junior staff.

> **Working parties/Project groups**

A meeting of people nominated to work on a specific task or project.

> **Steering meeting**

Meeting of a group that take an overview of a project. Not just the project team, this group may include senior members of staff and external people to help give a different viewpoint.

> **Team briefings**

A meeting for the supervisor or manager of a team to delegate tasks, discuss team issues and motivate the staff.

> **Exam board**

Meeting to report and discuss results of examinations.

> **Disciplinary board**

Special group to decide on action relating to an incident.

Also casual meetings on trains, in lifts, indeed any opportunity for a discussion.

Exercise:

What types of meetings do you attend?
How frequent are they?

....

....

....

....

....

....

....

Purposes and benefits of meetings

Exercise:

Why does your organization have meetings? Think of ten positive outcomes that have resulted from your meetings.

....

....

....

....

....

....

....

....

....

....

....

....

....

....

....

....

....

....

....

Ideas on the purposes and benefits of meetings

Meetings must have an objective. There is no point in having a meeting just because you always have one at 9am on a Tuesday morning if there is nothing to discuss.

Meetings can be used to:

✓ Share, discuss and exchange information - team work in action!

✓ Benefit from each other's views and opinions nobody should work in isolation – brainstorming ideas leads to more creativity.

✓ Decide upon the best action to take, as group discussion leads to more ideas.

✓ Analyze and solve problems by working with others to deal with work-based challenges.

✓ Talk about planned new developments and exchange ideas and suggestions for action. Giving different views and varying angles to reach the best possible solutions.

✓ Link together the activities undertaken by a number of people, ensuring people who are working on a project at different locations or in different offices are able to co-ordinate their activities.

✓ Discuss issues of mutual concern giving moral support.

✓ Exchange up to date information to make sure that everyone is aware of current events and developments. This communication leads to a happy and effective workforce. However, if the only purpose is to give information then is it better simply to send an email? If the topic isn't controversial, just send a note or put a notice on the intranet or a bulletin board.

✓ Plan the future of a project or company.

✓ Make decisions and come to an agreement.

✓ Review progress either to learn from the past or with a view to moving forward.

✓ Learn from the experience of fellow colleagues.

✓ Save time – as important issues can be debated with everyone concentrating on the same item at the same time. A well run meeting can ensure excellent time management.

✓ Increase understanding and appreciation of the views of other people. It is easy to be critical of other people and the way that they do things – having a meeting to understand each other's issues can improve relationships and communication.

✓ Reach the best possible conclusion, because the exchange of views and information leads to all the options being considered and the best one being chosen.

✓ Gain the commitment of those present on the decisions reached with witnesses!

✓ Allow staff to interact – particularly if they all work in different locations. This enhances communication – which makes an organization function effectively and efficiently.

Exercise: Do you have any other purposes and benefits for your particular meetings?

Why do we have minutes?

> **Exercise: In your workplace what are minutes used for?**

Minutes may be used for:

- ✓ Recording discussions
- ✓ Recording actions and enabling follow up
- ✓ Legal and/or audit purposes
- ✓ Informing people who were not at the meeting of anything of which they need to be aware
- ✓ Showing attendees (and apologies)
- ✓ Giving structure to the process

Key elements of a successful meeting

Requirements for a successful meeting:

✓ Meetings should be well organized, relevant and necessary.

✓ Attendees should be considerate, should listen to others – a mixture of people and skills helps.

✓ Attendees should have a positive attitude, that goes particularly for the minute taker .....

✓ NO MOBILE PHONES - we managed for thousands of years without them – it is possible to last out during a meeting without your phone on. If it is vital that people leave their mobile switched on, just make sure they leave to room to answer it. Sending texts during meetings shows disrespect for the people in the meeting.

✓ Hierarchy of needs are met – comfort, pleasant environment, etc. Make sure people are not too hot or cold, they've eaten and visited the washroom.

✓ A good chairperson.

Exercise: If you've attended meetings that didn't work what were the reasons?

....

....

....

....

....

....

....

What is the best meeting you've ever attended, and why?

....

....

....

....

....

....

....

Business meeting terms

> **Ad hoc**

Means "Arranged for this purpose."
Appointed to carry out one particular piece of work.
Sometimes they are called special or special purpose committees.

> **Any other business (AOB)**

At the end of a meeting there is often a section for items not covered by the rest of the agenda. These may either be by prior arrangement with the chair or they may be items brought forward by any member of the meeting without prior approval.

> **Adjournment**

Postponing the meeting because of lack of time or as further discussion needs to happen later.

> **Amendment**

A proposal to alter a motion by adding or deleting words.

> **Casting vote**

A second vote usually allowed to the chairman, except in the case of a company meeting. This is only used when there is an equal number of votes 'for' and 'against'.

> **Dissemination**

Spreading information widely.

> **Memorandum and articles of association**

Regulations drawn up by a company setting out the objects for which the company is formed and defining the manner in which its business shall be conducted.

> **Motion**

A question or a proposal – which when passed (approved) becomes a resolution.

> **No confidence**

When the members of a meeting disagree with the chair they pass a vote of 'no confidence' in the chair.

➤ **Point of order**

A question regarding the procedure at a meeting or a query relating to the standing orders or constitution.

➤ **Quorum**

The minimum number of persons who must be in attendance to constitute a meeting. This is stated in the constitution or rules of the organization. If there are enough people the meeting is then said to be 'quorate'.

➤ **Resolution**

A formal decision carried at a meeting.

➤ **Rider**

An additional clause or sentence added to a resolution after it has been passed (NB: it is an addition not an alteration).

➤ **Right of reply**

The proposer of a resolution has the right of reply when the resolution has been fully discussed.

➤ **Standing orders**

Rules compiled by the organization regulating the manner in which its business is to be conducted.

➤ **Status quo**

Used to refer to a matter in which there is to be no change.

➤ **Sub-committee**

Appointed by a committee to deal with some specific branch of its work.

➤ **Tabled**

If a document is tabled it is first seen at the meeting (brought to the table).

➤ **Terms of reference**

Why a meeting takes place – its purpose and objectives.

➤ **Unanimous**

When all members of a meeting have voted in favor of a resolution it is said to be carried unanimously.

Exercise: Are there any meeting terms used at work that you are not sure about, if so look them up now?

....

....

Item 2:
Preparation for a Meeting

"The best preparation for tomorrow is doing your best today." H. Jackson Brown Jr.

Item 2:
Preparation for a Meeting

Objectives for item 2, at the end of this item you will:

✓ Have an overview of the order of tasks that a minute taker might undertake

✓ Have examples of different types of agenda

✓ Know how to deal with documents that may be needed for a meeting

✓ Understand more about paperless meetings

In the section we are going to look at your role in preparing for the meeting. In many cases the person who takes the minutes is also responsible for preparing the agenda and liaising with the participants ahead of the meeting. First of all we will look at the order of tasks then at how to put the agenda together.

Order of tasks

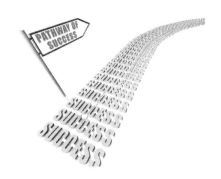

It is very rare that someone is asked to take minutes at a meeting without being involved in preparing for the meeting. In this book we are going to look at several of the stages that a minute taker might be involved with and at the back of the book is a checklist to help you make sure that you've completed each stage at the right time. On the following page is a chart showing each of the major stages you might be involved with.

Possible tasks for a minute taker

- ✓ Arrange meeting date, room and attendees
- ✓ Draft and agree the agenda
- ✓ Circulate the agenda and other meeting papers
- ✓ Prepare yourself, find out what the meeting is about
- ✓ Take notes at the meeting
- ✓ Write the minutes
- ✓ Check and proof the minutes
- ✓ Get approval for the minutes
- ✓ Circulate the minutes

Arranging the meeting

If it is your job to arrange the meeting location and resources then the following exercise will help.

Exercise: Planning your meeting

How many attendees will there be?
Who are the attendees?
What are their contact details?
Do any of them have special needs such as wheelchair access or an induction loop?
When should the meeting take place?
What style of seating do you need (boardroom, cabaret, lecture theater, circle of chairs)?
Is a seating plan needed?
What equipment do you need for any presentations?
Where is the best location?
What refreshments are needed?

Preparing agendas

Agendas serve several purposes. The main ones are keeping the meeting running in the correct sequence and covering the right topics. However, another major role of the agenda is to let the meeting participants know what the meeting will be about and also what it won't cover. If you are the person putting the agenda together and distributing it you'll need to work closely with the chair of the meeting to make sure the agenda is correct. You'll also need to get a list of who to circulate the agenda to, which may include some people who are not going to attend the meeting.

Agendas enable attendees to prepare for a meeting and should, therefore, be circulated in good time beforehand. You need to be aware of this for your planning. Remember, the agenda is also your first step to excellent preparation.

Styles of agenda

As you become more experienced, you can probably draft an agenda for the meeting. Until then, either ask the chairperson for topics or request suggestions from attendees. This draft can then be agreed with the chairperson.

The style of agendas can vary enormously. It is usually possible to find the agenda for a previous, similar meeting and use this format for the next meeting.

If there are several items on an agenda then number them. If an individual agenda item has more than one part then consider sub-section numbers, 2.1, 2.2, 2.3 etc.

Some agendas are very informal; they do not need to mention minutes of previous meetings or any other business.

Below is an example of an agenda for an ad hoc meeting.

From: A Manager
Sent: Friday 23 July 16:47
To: All staff
Subject: NEW IT SYSTEM

On 30 September, a new IT system is being introduced within the department. Training will be given to all staff as the method of working will be different.

In order that we can decide the best way to implement this training, I would like you to attend a brief meeting in my office at 9am on Wednesday 4th September. I expect the meeting to last about half an hour.

Please let me know immediately if, for any reason, you are unable to attend.

Tip: Always include the day of the week with the date, it helps avoid errors.

Here is an example of a more formal agenda:

EXPERT WINDOWS

HEALTH AND SAFETY COMMITTEE

The next meeting of the committee will be held in room G104 at 4pm on Wednesday 9th July 20XX.

1. Apologies

2. Minutes of the previous meeting

3. Matters arising

4. New building regulations

5. Planned IT updates

6. Any other business

7. Date and time of next meeting

Exercise:

Does your organization have anything different on its usual agendas? For instance: introductions or check in/ check out. (An insurance company I visited used this to motivate their meeting attendees.)

....

....

....

....

....

If you are going to be involved in organizing the agenda for a regular meeting it will be worth saving a copy as a basic structure (e.g. the meeting may always start with apologies, minutes of last meeting, matter arising and end with AOB and date of the next meeting).

When you become a more experienced minute taker, you may like to provide your chairperson with their own agenda. This is basically the same as the general agenda, but you can add information which would be of use to the chairperson in running the meeting. There is also space for the chair to make their own notes. You could also include proposed timings on this agenda.

A tip for laying out this style of agenda is to set it up as a table in word and then to set the border to none (usually in the format section). It can also be useful to use the bullet numbering system. Make sure the chair also has a copy of the simpler agenda given to the rest of the attendees.

You may like to make yourself a copy with even more space for notes.

Meeting	Health and Safety Committee	
Date/time	9 July 20XX at 4pm	
Place	G104, Expert College	

	AGENDA ITEM	NOTES
1	**Apologies for absence** Brian and Angela	1
2	**Minutes of the previous meeting**	2
3	**Matters Arising** Questions may be asked on results of recent drills	3
4	**New building regulations** Effective from 1/10/XX Copy circulated to members Surveyor's letter attached	4
5	**Planned IT updates** Scheduled for Oct/Nov Contractors: Ace Technology Directors' offices first	5
6	**Any other business** There may be questions on plans for bank holidays	6
7	**Date and time of next meeting** Suggest Wed 10th August	7

A completely different style is used for the agenda of an annual general meeting. If you don't use these in work, you may be familiar with them if you have a building society account and receive their annual statement and AGM agenda.

NOTICE OF MEETING

NOTICE IS HEREBY GIVEN that the sixty-sixth Annual General Meeting of the Insurance Company will be held at the Main Office of the Company at West Street, on Wednesday 24 July 20XX at 7pm for the purpose of transacting the following business.

AGENDA

1. To receive the Directors' Report, the Annual Accounts and the Auditors' Report thereon for the year ended 30 April 20XX.

2. To consider and, if thought fit, to pass the following Ordinary Resolutions:

> That West Audit plc be re-appointed as Auditors.
> That John Jones be re-elected as a Director.
> That Helen Smith be re-elected as a Director.

By Order of the Board of Directors

Alan Brown, Group Secretary, 16 June 20XX

Exercise: Collect examples of agendas from your organization. Have a critical look at them, how could you improve their content or style? Are there any common factors such as style or fixed items?

....

....

....

....

When to distribute

There is no set time to distribute an agenda, but ideally it should be sent out to give attendees (including the minute taker) enough time to prepare, but not so soon that it is out of date by the time of the meeting. It is difficult to give a recommended time because it very much depends on the 'speed' of the business. In many public organizations (hospitals, universities, etc), it is common to have an agenda one to two weeks before a meeting. This would rarely happen in fast moving business environments such as television or sales; within two weeks someone else could own your company!

Exercise: When do you distribute your agenda?
Is this the best time?

....

....

....

....

Exercise: What other papers do you need to distribute?

....

....

....

....

Do you already draft the agenda for the meetings you minute? If not, this might be the time to start. Let's look at some of the advantages of doing this:

➤ The agenda will be ready when you want it and this will give you time to prepare for the meeting. An effective minute taker cannot sit back and say "Well, I don't know what it's about.", you have to be proactive and find out what it's about.

➤ This will save the chairperson time and help them get their thoughts together. They may make changes to your draft but at least you have given them a starting point.

➤ It will enable you to have a better understanding of your organization's business.

➤ It can mean attendees also have more time to prepare.

➤ Attendees can give you suggestions for items to include.

Exercise: Can you think of any other reasons specific to your role?
....
....
....
....
....

Additional papers for the meeting

Extra reading for a meeting should be circulated with the agenda to give people plenty of opportunity to get through it. It needs to be kept to the bare minimum to avoid large amounts of photocopying. Also remember, if the pile of additional papers is too big people will avoid reading it.

Be creative - are there other ways of distributing the same information, for instance as web links or as pdf files?

If there are lots of papers for one meeting then you need to make sure that you organize them properly. Have a checklist for yourself to ensure you've included all the relevant papers. Label each paper with an easy to understand system. You may wish to include the document description on the agenda.

After the meeting, when you make your minutes it may be a good idea to add to the minutes where the document can be found for future reference.

Example of an agenda item with accompanying papers:

4. To decide on the color scheme for the new building.
See document 4.1, color pallet ideas for details.

The paperless meeting

In recent years technology has started to change the way we service meetings. Organizations are trying to move away from the massive amounts of paper that are generated, possibly unnecessarily, for meetings. Although some people may still be a long way from achieving this goal, there are many things which enable us to take the first steps.

Documents can be distributed before the meeting by email, using Dropbox (a single and generally secure place for all your data on the internet, which can be accessed from anywhere or any hardware) or shared drives. Microsoft Sharepoint, Broadview, GlobalMeet, WebEx, NetMeeting and Avaya are other options. Attendees should then take iPads, tablet PCs, laptops, smartphones, etc to the meeting. If you need to change the file format, for example from pdf to something like ePub, then there is a nice free bit of software called calibre (www.calibre-ebook.com).

It is also possible to review files, as a group, with Powerpoint, Microsoft Sharepoint and electronic white boards.

Meetings can be held as video or teleconferences, they can be held via Skype, Twitter, Adobe Connect, Microsoft Lync, Smart Phones and messaging systems.

Microsoft Cloud not only enables you to have all your social media, news and messaging in one place, you can also create photographs and films and then publish them. You can share high resolution photographs with photo email, you are given 25GB of free storage for files. For meetings, documents can be shared online and people can access their own information from anywhere.

It is now possible to take notes with a Livescribe smartpen. This computer in a pen records everything you write and everything you hear or say. You can replay your meetings by tapping on your notes and it takes you to what was being said at that moment. Livescribe paper is required and you can print off your own sheets on a laser printer.
(http://www.bakerwrite.com/cms/tools)

It combines a microphone, memory storage and infrared camera and the paper is printed with microdots. The pen records audio and tracks the pen on the page simultaneously. A micro-USB connector then transfers the notes and audio together to the desktop (and recharges the pen).

Research can be done instantly on the internet during meetings; it is important, however, to ensure that the internet doesn't become a distraction. A good chairperson will ensure control; a successful meeting does not occur if attendees are not focussed.

After the meeting, summaries can be typed up and distributed. Notes from Livescribe smartpens can be uploaded. Conversations on Twitter can reviewed.

What could you do to reduce or eliminate paper at your meetings?

....

....

....

....

Item 3:
Role and Skills of the Minute Taker

"Success is simple.
Do what's right, the right way, at the right time."
Arnold H. Glasgow

Item 3:
Role and Skills of the
Minute Taker

Objectives for item 3, at the end of this item you will:

✓ Have a definition of the role of the minute taker

✓ Know 10 skills required to be an effective minute taker

✓ Have considered your level of skill in these areas

✓ Have completed exercises to practice some of the skills

Role of the minute taker

What exactly is the role of the minute taker? As one manager once said to me, "you just go in and take notes, don't you?" If only it were so simple.

The minute taker's role is frequently perceived as easy and something any administrator can do (and, I'm afraid I have seen many examples of the role falling to the only woman in a meeting as though being a 34C means you have natural ability to take notes!)

The role of the minute taker should not include making refreshments during the meeting – what would happen about the notes? It does not include running in and out to take photocopies, fetch reports, etc – same question. It certainly does not include being bullied.

This is, I believe, the best definition I have seen:

> **The role of the minute taker is to produce a document, for several other people to read, which summarizes the meeting and actions to be taken.**

The person carrying out that role should be given full support to do the job effectively.

Exercise: Are there any tasks you are asked to perform which inhibit your ability to carry out the role of minute taker?

....

....

....

....

....

....

....

....

....

....

....

....

....

....

....

Now in order to carry out your role effectively you need to think about the skills required and this is what we are going to concentrate on for the rest of this chapter.

Skills required for taking minutes

> ➢ **Being good at taking notes**

You should have your own prepared system for taking quick notes and it should include a set of abbreviations. Remember you don't need to write perfect English in the meeting. Prepare your abbreviations in advance of the meeting. If you haven't already got a system have a look at the BakerWrite system of speed writing (www.UoLearn.com). Make sure you work out how you will differentiate between people with the same initials before you go into the meeting.

> ➢ **Good mastery of English**

This is very important so that people can understand your minutes and to reflect a good image of you, your department and organization.

> ➢ **Good vocabulary**

You'll need a good general vocabulary and an understanding of the technical terms, jargon and abbreviations that may be used in the meeting. Get yourself informed before the meeting so you'll understand what's being said. Use a thesaurus to vary the words you use.

> ➢ **Word processing skills**

A set of well presented minutes reflects well on you. If you are regularly minuting the same type of meeting then use a template. You can then use a laptop and type your notes straight onto your template – but remember you are not writing your minutes in the meeting, you are just taking notes.

> ➢ **Summarizing skills**

This is after the meeting, you need to write a summary based on the notes you have taken.

> **Listening skills**

Always the first skill that people think of as the most difficult.

> **Proofreading skills**

It's important to check your minutes after they have been typed.

> **Knowledge of how to use reported speech**

You may occasionally have to report what people say in minutes and, if so, reported speech should be used (more later). However, by using excellent summarizing skills you can avoid the 'he said, she said' scenarios.

> **A good relationship with the Chairperson**

A very important part of minute taking – this will be discussed in detail later.

> **What to record**

A sense of what you should and shouldn't record is a skill that takes time to develop. It helps to understand your readership and the use of the minutes after they have been written.

Exercise: Rate your own abilities at the skills of a minute taker on a scale of 1 to 5. With 1 being very poor ability and 5 being an excellent command of this skill.

	1	2	3	4	5
Note taking	☹	○	😐	○	☺
English mastery	☹	○	😐	○	☺
Good vocabulary	☹	○	😐	○	☺
Word processing	☹	○	😐	○	☺
Summarizing	☹	○	😐	○	☺
Listening	☹	○	😐	○	☺
Proofreading	☹	○	😐	○	☺
Reported speech	☹	○	😐	○	☺
Working with chair	☹	○	😐	○	☺
What to record	☹	○	😐	○	☺

We are now going to give you tips on how to improve. Concentrate on practicing those where you feel you need help.

Note taking

Another delegate's 'horror story' was that when she took notes at her company's board meetings, the Board members sat around a large table and she was made to sit at a separate table, in a corner, with her back to everyone! When I recovered from the shock of hearing this, thinking what an awful way to treat a colleague and how many ways the poor woman was prevented from effectively carrying out her role, I asked why she had to have her back to everyone. Wait for it ..... it was apparently for 'confidentiality'! I know, this answer led to more questions than any clarity. I suggested they could have put a bag over her head instead ......

As you read this book, just think about that lady and how, in every way, she was prevented for carrying her out role.

Here are some tips to help you:

✓ Sit somewhere where there are few or no distractions. Hopefully the meeting room will be in a quiet location and ideally the minute taker should sit next to the chairperson. If you sit at the opposite end of the table then the discussion will be taking place away from you (towards the chairperson) and this will make it more difficult for you to hear and therefore take notes. Also the minute taker and the chairperson should be running the meeting together and should be able to communicate quickly and easily. A quick nudge if the meeting is running late....

✓ Have a spare pen or pencil and plenty of paper or use your laptop. The basics, but very important for your efficiency. If you do have access to a laptop or there is a computer in the meeting room, you can type your notes directly onto your minutes template (we will come back to this later). Also, remember, you are typing notes NOT your minutes. Whether you are using a laptop or a pen, do make sure you are not wearing distracting jewellery or watches that make a noise against the table as you type/write. This, and long nails on keyboards, can be very distracting for the other attendees.

✓ Get as much information as possible about the meeting beforehand so you will understand what is being said.

As a minute taker you can't just sit back and say "I don't know what's going on"; you have to be proactive in getting yourself informed. However, you do need support for this too.
Let's have a think about the sort of things you could do to get informed:

➢ Read the previous minutes – you may have typed them, but it could have been a month ago, or even 3 months ago. A quick look through will remind you of what happened last time and help you understand the meeting.
   If it's your first time minuting this meeting then this is a good initial way to get yourself informed.

➢ Read any papers that are to be distributed – yes, I realize this takes time and you are very busy; however, just a quick skim of the documents could save you stress and a lot of time in the long run – it's worth it. You will at least get an idea of what is being discussed and you will also be able to see what words may come up and find out what they mean, how they are spelled and how you may abbreviate them.

➢ Have a meeting with the chairperson; this is essential before a meeting as you should be working as a team to run a successful meeting. The chair can then give you information about topics and tell you the sort of things you should be noting down.

➢ Have meetings with attendees, experts, other minute takers – all these people can give you information and support, but you must be assertive to ensure they give you their time.

➢ Use available information sources such as the internet, your organization's intranet, newspapers, TV, radio, etc. Keep yourself up to date with the world of your business.

➢ 'Ears and eyes' – basically what you do to learn your role – keeping your ears and eyes open and picking up on things that may come up in meetings. Reading emails, notices, listening to conversations, etc.

➢ Draft the agenda yourself and check with the chairperson; you will then know what topics are due to be discussed and can start your research sooner.

Exercise: Is there anything else could you do to get yourself informed for your meetings?

....

....

....

....

What do you write in your notes?

➢ **Decide or check beforehand how detailed the notes should be**

Speak to the chairperson and establish how detailed the minutes should be; this means you will know how detailed your notes should be.

➢ **Look at the speakers**

You can hear people much better, and therefore find it easier to take notes, if you look at the speakers. "But", I hear you ask, "how can we be looking at the speakers if we're taking notes?" Well, the next point makes this clear and is probably one of the most important parts of this book.

➢ **MINUTE TAKING IS NOT DICTATION**

Dictation is when someone dictates a note and you type it back in full, word for word. Minute taking is about listening and then jotting down key words that will remind you of what happened. This gets much easier as you become more experienced. The main tips for this are ......

➢ **Don't launch in**

Don't start writing immediately people start speaking otherwise you will end up writing a lot of words you don't need, then getting behind and that leads to panic.

Just wait a few minutes until you get the gist of the conversation and then write down the words that will remind you of what was said.

> **Leave out small words (e.g. a, the, in, etc) if the meaning is clear**

Your good English skills matter less in note taking; you don't need to write your notes in beautifully constructed sentences with perfect spelling – do that when you type up your minutes. Remember, in the meeting you are taking notes; you write your minutes after the meeting. One of the main reasons people get in a panic in minute taking is because they try to write their minutes in the meeting and this is not possible.

So full sentences are not needed here and miss out any unnecessary small words (don't leave out 'not', that's usually pretty important!).

> **Use contractions, abbreviations and initials**

Develop your own shorthand for often used words and phrases (if you don't already take notes in shorthand). Learn a speed writing system (see www.UoLearn.com) if you don't already do shorthand; this will give you a structure for your quick writing. If you make up abbreviations during the meeting you probably won't be able to read them back afterwards.

> **Review and type up your notes as quickly as possible after the meeting**

The sooner you type up the notes, the quicker you will finish them. Every day you leave them makes them more difficult to transcribe as your memory of the meeting fades – not good time management.

Remember – how do you eat an elephant?

One piece at a time!

If you're very busy don't try and do your minutes all in one go; just make a start and keep coming back to them.

A very important tip here – you should not try and write your minutes in the meeting. In the meeting you are taking notes, you write your minutes (the summary) after the meeting.

I think this is one of the main reasons minute takers get in such a panic during meetings as they are trying to do two jobs at once.

Exercise: Have a practice at taking notes from real meetings.
http://www.youtube.com/watch?v=fXluP2vjNiw
http://www.youtube.com/watch?v=WahloApfLmI
(just as far as you want to - it does go on a while)

Some more general tips for note taking:

➢ Always keep your writing small and close together; you will write faster because your pen spends less time on the paper.

➢ Don't press too hard; you will become more physically tired.

➢ Don't use capital letters; block capitals are much slower to produce.

➢ Don't write too close to the edges of the paper; this prevents faster writing because you have to slow down near the edges.

➢ If you're using an A4 notepad, fold the page in half lengthways and write down one side and then the other; because you have less space you will automatically write less.

➢ If you are using a small ring bound notepad, as you near the bottom of a page, start to push the paper up and then flip over as you reach the end.

➢ Use your non-writing hand to fold over the bottom corner of your pad to enable a quick flip (see above) and hence faster writing!

➢ Learn a system of speed writing; BakerWrite takes just 6 hours to learn and only a few weeks to become proficient (with regular practice).

Exercise: Find a colleague who has written minutes and ask for their 3 best tips.

....

....

....

A good mastery of English

Why is good English included in the list of skills required?

If we go back to the role of the minute taker, we said that he/she must produce a document for several other people to read – well, they have to understand it.

It is also important that during the meeting you understand what people are saying. You need to consider that what you write reflects well on you, your department, your chairperson and your organization if the minutes are well written.

For more help with this try
Write Right!, Jan Venolia, ISBN 9781580083287
Mastering English Grammar, S.H.Burton, ISBN 9780333363683
Idiot's Guide to Grammar and Style, L.Rozakis, 9780028619569

So let's go over some of the basics that people get wrong.

Answers to most of the exercises in this section are at the back of the book.

Grammar

A verb is a doing word, eg, to dance, to eat, to have, etc.

Verbs usually go after the name of the person or object that is undertaking the action.

Eg: Peter **went** home on his motorbike.
Tina **was washing** her windows.
He **jumped** on the trampoline.

In the basic (or infinite version) you use the word to in front of the verb.

to walk, to see, to climb, to say

Verbs change their endings depending on what is undertaking the action and when it happened. They are often accompanied by parts of the verb to be (is, was, were). The three endings for regular verbs (ones that follow the rules) are:

s , ing and ed

I open the door. Paul open**s** the door. Hamid open**ed** the door.
Sid **is** open**ing** the door. Sarah **was** open**ing** the door.

Every sentence must have a verb. Sometimes, in modern text layouts, bullet points are used where the verb is given at the start and not included in each bullet point, but there should still be a verb. E.g.

We need to consider:

- The past year's accounts

- The current income

- Next year's projected income

Another important point about verbs is that the tense (which part of the verb to use) should be consistent throughout a set of minutes. If you look at the following you'll see how it doesn't work.

I **went** to a meeting and I **am buying** the materials from it. I **met** Sandra. She **is telling** me that there **is** another meeting next month.

This is clearly about a trip made in the past so all the verbs should agree and be about the past. So it should read:

I **went** to a meeting and I **bought** the materials from it. I **met** Sandra. She **told** me that there **will be** another meeting next month.

If you are writing minutes most of the report will be in the past tense. The only parts that will not be are predictions about future actions. None of it should be in the present tense.

Once you've written your minutes you need to check that the verbs are correct. One of the best ways to of this is to read them out aloud. (Try this with the example above.) Unfortunately grammar checkers will not pick it up.

An adverb describes how a verb was done.

He walked **quickly**. The rain was falling **heavily.**

A noun is a naming word this covers a wide variety, eg, table, Manchester, he, she, life, feeling, etc

Nouns are often preceded by a, an (if they start with a vowel) and the.

the house, a mouse, an elephant,

When writing minutes you need to be careful that it is clear which person or object you are referring to. So sometimes it is appropriate to use impersonal pronouns (ones that don't repeat what the noun is) such as he, she, they or it. However, you need to be careful that the reader can work out who you mean.

Bad example: MJ said that PL should have found the accounts from last year. **He** said that this was an important task and that he would do it.

So now, who has agreed to do the task MJ or PL from these minutes? It could be either of them. If more than one person is involved it is usually better to repeat the name of the person involved.

MJ said that PL should have found the accounts from last year. **PL** said that this was an important task and that he would do it.

Nouns should only start with capital letters if they are the name of a specific object or person (proper nouns).

For example, London, New York, July, John.

They should not be used for emphasis only.

Adjectives describe nouns, such as colors and size.

The **blue** sky was above a **large** tree.

> Exercise: Pick out the verb(s), noun(s) and adjective(s) in the following sentences.
>
> 1. The usual chairperson read the minutes.
> 2. It was agreed to increase the annual salaries.
> 3. Mr Smith volunteered to send an explanatory email.
> 4. KL said that he would try out the new system.

Problem words:

Many of the words people struggle to spell have two variants with similar sounding alternatives and to make matters worse UK and US spellings can be reversed.

Examples of this are practice/practise and license/licence. As a rule of thumb, look for the use of 'the' and 'a' for a noun and 'ing' and 'ed' endings for a verb.

A really good way to remember other alternatives is to develop a strong memory for the correct spelling by making a connection between the correct spelling and something that makes sense to you (see the next page for some examples).

Words often spelled incorrectly in minutes:

Accommodation	Effect, usually noun	Practice (UK noun, US noun and verb)
Accomplish	Environment	Practise (verb, UK only)
Achieve	Further	Preferred
Acquire	Government	Receive
Address	Guarantee	Recommend
Affect (verb)	Immediately	Referred
Business	Independent	Separate
Colleague	Liaise/liaison	Stationary (not moving)
Commitment	Licence (noun, UK only)	Stationery (paper)
Committee	License (verb)	Success
Comparative	Necessary	Unforeseen
Conceive	Occasion	Withhold
Consensus	Opportunity	
Correspondence	Permanent	

A tip for UK spellers - if you're trying to decide c or s in practice or licence then try saying the words advice and advise instead. They work the same way as practice/practise.

Some examples of how you can remember some of these spellings:

affect = verb, How will this affect us?
I was affected by the music. The noise was affecting my performance

effect = noun (usually), The effect was serious. An effect of these problems is....

station**a**ry = not moving; not **active**
station**e**ry = papers, pens, etc (remember e for **envelope**)

princi**pal** = head of something, e.g. school principal, a person could be your **pal** also means the main reason
princi**ple** = an idea, an **excellent** idea

comp**le**ment = it **completes** something
comp**li**ment = a nice comment, use a compliment to **impress**

If you visit http://www.askoxford.com/betterwriting/spelling/?view=uk you'll find lots more useful tips.

Exercise: Are there any words you know you always mix up? If so, look up the correct version and think of a memory link to help you remember the spelling.

....
....
....
....
....

Exercise: Select the correct spelling from the options given in these sentences:

1. He had been practising/practicing medicine for years.
2. It was a nice compliment/complement about my work.
3. The principal/principle reason why the project succeeded was the team management.
4. The chairperson was concerned about the affect/effect this would have on the practise/practice time.

Punctuation

➢ Full stop (.)

A full stop used at the end of a sentence and is always followed by a capital letter. In the past, full stops were placed after all abbreviations; nowadays they are rarely used. This is called open punctuation. We know what 'etc', 'ie' or 'Mr' are.

➢ Commas

A comma (,) - denotes a pause in a sentence and can be used to break up items in a list.

If you write a list, all of the items should be separated by commas apart from the last two which should have and between them:

Our business last year sold widgets, gadgets, shapes **and** thingamabobs.

If you are writing long sentences then commas separate clauses. A clause is a part of the sentence that could be removed and the sentence still make sense. A clause usually gives more detailed information. There needs to be a comma at the start and end, unless the clause ends the sentence.

Examples:

At the meeting, **which was on Friday,** we decided to go ahead with project. **However,** it was decided that it wouldn't start until February.

So you could remove the clauses to get:

At the meeting we decided to go ahead with project. It was decided that it wouldn't start until February.

Which still make sense.

What's the difference between a cat and a comma?
A cat has claws at the end of its paws and
a comma is a pause at the end of a clause!

51

➢ **Colons (:)**

Colons are used to denote the start of a list, often where the items within it are more than one word long. Traditionally after a colon all the items in the list are separated by semi-colons(;). However, modern usage is that they are often used to start bullet lists and the end punctuation is often not put in.

Traditional
There are four reasons for the project working: the team worked well together; the price of widgets rose; the price of electricity fell and none of the equipment failed.

Modern
There are four reasons for the project working:
1. The team worked well together
2. The price of widgets rose
3. The price of electricity fell
4. None of the equipment failed

➢ **Semi-colons (;)**

Semi-colons are used to separate complicated lists (see above). They can also be used to denote two separate thoughts in the same sentence; if in doubt, use a full stop.

➢ **Exclamation marks (!)**

Exclamation marks should be used to denote surprise in a voice. He said, "Watch out!" However, they are now often used to denote irony and humor. As a suggestion most minutes are about serious meetings and the advice is not to use exclamation marks at all.

➢ **Questions marks (?)**

Should be used to denote an asked question. Again, these would not be used in minutes as you are not writing to someone and, therefore, would not be asking a question.

➢ **Brackets (())**

Brackets can be used as an alternative to commas, often they indicate an extra thought associated with but not necessary to the sentence, such as (see the previous minutes).

> ## Apostrophes (')

The apostrophe is perhaps the most misunderstood of all punctuation and yet can be vital to complete clarity.

The apostrophe has 2 functions:

1.   Contractions

2.   Possession

Contractions

The apostrophe is used to indicate the missing letter(s), eg:

She's told him = She has told him

I'm here = I am here

I can't = I cannot

I wouldn't = I would not

We aren't = We are not

Words to watch out for:

your = belonging to you
you're = you are

there = over there
their = belonging to them
they're = they are

its = belonging to it
it's = it is or it has
(its' does not exist)

If you are not sure which to use try replacing **it's** by **it is** if it works you need the apostrophe, if it doesn't you don't need one.

It's finished now. It is finished now.

Its door was red. It is door was red - this doesn't work so no apostrophe is correct - the door belonging to something was red.

You must note, however, that contractions are not usually used in very formal minutes. If you're not sure have a chat with your chair.

Possession

When the possessor is single (ie, just one person or thing), we indicate possession by using an apostrophe followed by the letter s:
The director's report
My manager's project
The lady's desk

When the possessors are plural (ie, more than one person or thing), we indicate possession by placing an apostrophe after the final s:
The executives' conference
My colleagues' attitude
The secretaries' desks

However, when a word changes completely in the plural, the apostrophe remains before the s:
The men's books
The children's facilities
The women's bags.

If the subject is followed by a verb an apostrophe will probably not be needed, if it is followed by a noun then one may be required.

If you have a word with an s in it and you're not sure whether it needs an apostrophe try replacing the s with the words belonging to and put the noun first.

The director's car.
The car belonging to the director.
So, the apostrophe is needed as this works.

The directors sat in the car.
The car belonging to the directors sat in.
This makes no sense at all so the apostrophe is not needed, the s here just means more than one director. Also car is a noun and sat is a verb.

Apostrophes are not required where there is no possession eg:

The PAs visited the seminar.
The PCs were working well.
She was born in the 1960s.

Exercise: Add any missing apostrophes.

1. The clients rooms are nearby. (three clients)

2. The managers response was "no". (one manager)

3. The secretaries attitude must improve.

4. The mens preference was to sit down.

5. The caretaker says that hes happy with this plan.

6. Youre not sure what your choice will be.

7. Its difficult to know if the company and its representatives are included.

8. The SATs were very difficult.

A good vocabulary

There are different aspects of vocabulary that are important in minute taking. You need to have a good variety of words that you can use so that you are not always repeating the same ones (such as he said, she said , then she said). You also need to have a working vocabulary for your specialist area.

Words that could be used in minute taking

The following groups of words cannot be used as synonyms, but may be useful as alternatives to avoid repetition.

said stated reported established confirmed added commented verified declared pointed out	explained acknowledged suggested described understood advised highlighted drew attention to outlined reported	raised informed were reminded that recalled emphasized clarified illustrated defined demonstrated indicated
planned intended meant hoped proposed	benefits of merits of advantages of worth value of	problems drawbacks dangers uncertainty disadvantages
options alternatives choice preference opportunity	worried concerned troubled uneasy anxious apprehensive	decided resolved approved concluded determined

disagreed disputed not the case	agreed concurred	potential possibility likelihood prospect chance probability
discussed debated deliberated considered examined analyzed	existence of issue of reality of topic of problem of question of challenge of	chose opted selected picked named preferred
discussed the problems with the existence of challenges in the extent of issues in		
the probability of issues in the potential for problems in the possibility of challenges in		
No action necessary No decision taken No consensus reached	Deferred to [date] Referred to [person/group]	

Always use a thesaurus to check that you are not altering the meaning of the text. A good online version is www.thesaurus.com

Exercise: Re-write the following paragraph to avoid repetition and to flow better.

It was agreed that there was a very good chance that the manager would tell the department what she was going to do. The chairperson said that the CEO had said that everyone should be told about the fact that there could well be redundancies. She also said that she thought this would happen.

Know your own in-house vocabulary

Any working environment has its own special words and acronyms (letters that represent something like NATO or USA) and as minute taker you must use and understand these terms.

If they are more widely used acronyms you can use something like www.acronymfinder.com to help. However, if they are local terms then you've only got one option:

IF YOU DON'T KNOW ASK!

The best way to approach this is to develop your own personal dictionary. Either ask in the meeting or afterwards, but certainly before you send out the minutes.

Word	Meaning

Word processing

Tip: If you don't know how to do something on your computer look it up on youtube. You'll be surprised how much is there.

How to create a minutes template in word from an existing (or blank) document:

1. Open your existing (or blank) document and ensure you only have the aspects of the minutes that occur for every meeting.
2. Go to File then Save as.
3. When you get the dialogue box go to the line Save as type, it will say 'word document'. Click on the down arrow and select "document template". The Save in at the top of the box will default to the 'Templates' directory.
4. Call your template something appropriate (eg, Board minutes).
5. Click on Save.
6. Close template. When you want to create your next minutes, go to File then New from template and select the one you want.
7. Save this as a normal word document (eg, January board minutes).
8. Next time you open the template again and don't have to delete all the text from your previous minutes.

Please note that with Vista the default in point 3 does not work; it enables you to save in any file. You will need to investigate your system to find out where your templates should be located.

Examples of what may go in your template:

➢ Formatting
➢ Title
➢ Regular agenda items
➢ (Attendees)
➢ (Location)

Exercise: Can you think of anything else to add to your template specific to your minutes?

....

....

You can also then start typing your minutes in advance of the meeting. There are some things which don't go in your template, but which you do know before the meeting:

Other agenda headings

Presentations

Apologies

Exercise: Anything else to add for your minutes?

....

....

....

....

....

....

File care

Before you start make sure you have a good system in which to store your files. It is important that you have a systematic method for naming your files for minutes. A suggestion would be to include the meeting name and date in the file heading. Such as projectcommitminutes05062014. Including the date is very helpful as it makes sure each file has a unique name so you don't overwrite previous files and it also means if you are hunting for a particular meeting later you can find it more quickly. If the minutes have to be sent round to several people before you publish them then add v1, v2, final at the end of the file name to make sure you know which version you are working on.

Make sure your system is set to back your work up on a regular basis.

Listening skills for minute taking

The four steps of listening:

➢ **Hearing**

This is being aware of sounds, but not concentrating on what is happening.

➢ **Interpretation**

Now you're thinking carefully about what you are hearing. Your past experiences, culture, attitudes and vocabulary will affect how you interpret it.

➢ **Evaluation**

You are now deciding what to do with the information you have heard; you are making judgments.

➢ **Response**

You are now listening. You now respond to what you have heard. In minute taking it is deciding what to put in your notes.

How to become a better listener in meetings:

➢ **Don't talk – listen.**

Ideally the minute taker shouldn't be involved in the meeting, although often they may also have another role at the meeting too. If you do have to do both, it is helpful if the chairperson gives you a moment to make notes between items of discussion and so then you can take part in the discussion effectively.

➢ **Don't assume you know what people are going to say.**

The person who usually says nothing of any importance may come up with their best idea yet! Keep an open mind.

➢ **Focus on content not delivery.**

Although body language is a vital part of understanding what people mean; in minute taking you have to write what people said. Also, don't let people's accents or mannerisms distract you.

➢ **Drink plenty of water.**

One of the main reasons for lack of concentration is dehydration – have a glass of water handy (much better than coffee or fizzy drinks).

➢ **Understand the issues being discussed**

Refer back to the earlier issue of note taking.

➢ **Encourage the Chairperson to ensure attendees don't all talk at once**

A minute taker is often only as good as their chairperson. It is impossible to minute a meeting where everyone is talking at once or in small groups. If your chair tends to let this happen, in your pre-meeting with them, you might like to ask what they would like you to do if everyone starts talking at once – raising awareness of the issue. Hopefully they will offer to keep control of the meeting.

➢ **Be motivated**

To get the most out of a meeting go in with a positive attitude. Say to yourself, "What can I learn from this to make me more valuable to my company?" You might be surprised at what you can learn, even from routine meetings and chats at the drinking fountain!

Barriers to listening:

➢ **Inner struggles**

If you have serious worries, it may be better to ask someone else to take the minutes. However, often we just have to get on with things. You must say to yourself that while you are in the meeting there is nothing you can do about your problem and so put it to the back of your mind.

➢ **Lack of knowledge**

You now know what to do to get informed (see the section on agendas).

➢ **Accents and mumbling**

Get mumblers to sit near to you.

Ask the chairperson to raise awareness of the fact that you need to hear properly.

Email people afterwards with your proposed text and ask them to check if you've understood correctly.

Check with the chairperson about what has been said.

Ask, if appropriate (see assertiveness skills later).

➢ **Overload**

It is very frustrating to have to go into a meeting to take minutes when your in-tray is overflowing. If you sit in the meeting worrying about it you are not doing either job properly. So, decide before the meeting what you are going to do about your work (maybe stay later). Then forget about it and focus on the meeting.

➢ **Timing**

If you have any say at all in when a meeting will happen, make sure it suits you.

➢ **Fatigue**

If you know you're minuting a meeting the next day, make sure you get a good night's sleep.

Summarizing skills – writing the minutes

What is summarizing? It is writing concise minutes, not necessarily missing things out, but what you do write you write in as short a way as possible.

> ➢ **Identify key points**

We'll look at this in more depth in the what to record section.

> ➢ **Don't include examples or descriptions used simply to illustrate a particular point**

When people speak they make a point and then usually give examples to illustrate that point. For the minutes you only need the key point.

Some of you may have read John Fowles' novels ("The French Lieutenant's Woman", "The Magus"); he is a very descriptive writer and, if someone walks through the door, he would probably describe the door frame, the door handle, etc. In fact, for the story, we only need to know that the guy has walked through the door. It is the same for minutes.

> ➢ **Arrange information into a logical order**

The minutes should always been written in the same order as the agenda, even if the meeting actually happened in a different order.

Also, within each agenda point, people will go in all directions with the discussion. Your notes may be in no particular order. When you come to type your minutes you should ensure your notes are well structured and logical. Nobody wants a rehash of the whole meeting.

And, remember, you are not summarizing in the meeting, you are taking notes in the meeting and summarizing afterwards. If you've any doubt as to whether something should be included, just put it in your notes and decide later when you're calmer and have more time to think. (Minute taking is not dictation.)

> ➢ **Keep to the facts – don't include opinions**

This is not you saying, "and I thought this was a load of rubbish!". This is where you use words that give away your opinion. For example, "there was a lengthy discussion". How long is "lengthy"? About 5 minutes on the afternoon before the weekend!

In an exercise about people taking examinations, that I did with my trainees, someone on my course wrote, "Mr Fish said that exams were looming." At no point was the word 'looming' used in the meeting. This just shows that the minute taker didn't like exams! Best of all, how about the person who wrote, "it was eventually decided"; how brassed off was that minute taker?

> **Check grammar, spelling, punctuation**

At this point your grammar, etc should be perfect.

> **Do not write in note form – use proper sentences**

I'm not saying don't use bullets; they are fine. However, you should write in full sentences, this is what gives your minutes clarity – and elegance.

> **Avoid repetition**

We've already looked at not repeating the same words, but we must also think about not saying the same phrases more than once. Often, in a meeting, people will say things 3 or 4 times, possibly using different words. You may have some points in your notes more than once. When you come to write your minutes, make sure it's only in once.

> **Don't go through 'the process'**

This is what can make minutes extremely long-winded – see the following example:

The Chairperson said she needed a volunteer to get estimates for the new furniture in the office. She asked the Secretary to do this. The Secretary said she would do this. The Chairperson said she needed these for the next meeting. The Secretary said she would arrange this.

This could have been better written as follows:

The Secretary agreed to arrange estimates for the new furniture to be discussed at the next meeting.

One delegate on my course, who I saw on another course a year or so later, told me that she had reduced her minutes from twenty pages to two! She said she always used to take down everything that everybody said and then just type it up (dictation!). She told me she was now summarizing and that people were actually reading her minutes. She realized this because previously nobody had ever made any comments on them and now they were.

Now you have a go:

Exercise: Think of ways to improve these phrases and avoid repetition.

1. Jon Smith (JS) brought the sales figures to the meeting. These were distributed to the members of the Committee and discussed and Jane Adams (JA) agreed they had improved. All other attendees agreed they had improved too. It was agreed that a bonus could be paid this year.

2. The repairs needed to the new offices were discussed. It was quite rightly agreed that the walls needed painting, the windows needed replacing and the doors needed replacing. Mr Jones agreed to contact the Board to get their permission to carry out these repairs.

3. JS asked the Committee for their views on the proposed new pay system. JA said she thought it was good, HB said he thought there some issues which should be looked at in more detail. JS and JA agreed with this. These issues were then discussed and everyone then agreed that they would go ahead with this new system.

4. The Committee discussed the half year sales figures ending 30th June. It was noted that a profit of £13 million had been made in the first 6 months of the year.

Proofreading

CANDIDATE FOR A PULLET SURPRISE

I have a spelling checker,
It came with my PC.
It plane lee marks four my revue
Miss steaks aye can knot sea.

Eye ran this poem threw it,
Your sure reel glad two no.
Its vary polished in it's weigh.
My checker tolled me sew.

A checker is a bless sing,
It freeze yew lodes of thyme.
It helps me right awl stiles two reed,
And aides me when eye rime.

Each frays come posed up on my screen
Eye trussed too bee a joule.
The checker pours o'er every word
To cheque sum spelling rule.

Bee fore a veiling checker's
Hour spelling mite decline,
And if we're lacks oar have a laps,
We wood bee maid too wine.

Butt now bee cause my spelling
Is checked with such grate flare,
Their are know fault's with in my cite,
Of nun eye am a wear.

Now spelling does knot phase me,
It does knot bring a tier.
My pay purrs awl due glad den
With wrapped word's fare as hear.

To rite with care is quite a feet
Of witch won should bee proud,
And wee mussed dew the best wee can,
Sew flaw's are knot aloud.

Sow ewe can sea why aye dew prays
Such soft wear four pea seas,
And why eye brake in two averse
Buy righting want too pleas.

Written by Jerrold Zar and reprinted with kind permission of
The Journal of Irreproducible Results,
The science humor magazine, www.jir.com

Often administrative staff are so busy that little time is spent on checking work. However, just taking a few more minutes to both check and proofread what you have typed can save you so much time in the long run – and possibly embarrassment.

Here are some tips for checking the content of your minutes:

✓ Good layout and presentation
✓ Key points only (no examples)
✓ Clear and concise
✓ Short and simple sentences
✓ No superfluous information
✓ Logical order
✓ Date, time, venue; next meeting, etc
✓ Attendees
✓ Action points, person responsible and deadline
✓ Facts (no opinions!)
✓ Papers discussed
✓ Vary vocabulary and avoid repetition

Try to leave at least a couple of hours between checking and proofreading your work as it will help you find errors.

Here is a checklist for proofreading your minutes (looking for typos):

❑ Check on the screen before you print off, but ALWAYS check again from the printed version

❑ Don't just check the text, remember headings, layout and the action column too

❑ Are there any missing words?

❑ Read 'out loud' to slow you down

❑ Don't rely on spellcheck – use a dictionary and thesaurus too

❑ Full sentences, full stops, capital letters

❑ Correct grammar, spelling and punctuation

❑ Past tense, reported speech, 3rd person

Exercise: Now have a go at proofreading this extract from some minutes:

1. Apologies for absence
    No apologies were recieved.

2. Minutes of the last meeting
    The Chairperson asked members to correct a typing erro in item 3.1, as the the figure of £11,200 should read £ 111,200. After this amendment, the minutes were approved and signed by the Chairperson as a correct record.

3. Matters arising
    Their were no matters arising.

4. Chairperson's report
    The Chairperson pointed out taht over the last 6 months membership had fallen by 20%. She felt that this was due largly to lack of pubilcity during the present year, and also that new employes were not aware of how to join. The following decisions were reached:
    4.1 Circular to all staff
    A letter would be sent from the Chairperson to all employees who were not members fo the Club. This letter would outline it's aims and activities. A tear-off slip would be included for employees to indicated any areas of interest.   CW
    4.2 Social evening
    A social evening would be organized specfically for non-members, to include refreshments. Miss Chen agreed to make the arrangments.   CC

5. New aerobics classes
    Miss Carol Chen proposed that aerobics classes should be held. Mrs Sharon Warner from the Cool Gym had agreed to conduct these classes on the Companys premises every Wenesday evening from 6-7pm.
    Miss Chen will provide further information.   CW

1. Any other business
    There was no other business.

Two others things to check when you are proofreading is that you use past tense and third person.

Past tense

Minutes should always be written in the past tense. You are reporting on what happened in the meeting, not on what the situation is currently.

An exception to this would be actions, where you may use the future tense. Try and avoid the very clumsy and inelegant use of 'to do something' in actions. For example, "Mr Jones to send an email". It's the same number of words to say "Mr Jones will send an email" or "Mr Jones offered to send an email." As well as being grammatically correct, it is also much easier to read.

Third person

Formal minutes should always been written in the third person. That is using he, she or it, or Mr Jones, Bob or the Personnel Director.

Third person plural is they or the members of the committee.

In formal minutes you should never use I, we, you, me, my, us, our or your.

- ✗ It was agreed that, as an organization, we did not have a very good policy on health and safety.
- ✓ It was agreed that the organization did not have a very good policy on health and safety.

Reported speech

"I agree," said the chairperson – this is an example of quoted or direct speech; this should never be used in minutes.

We should not quote people but we should report what they say, hence 'reported speech'.

For example: The chairperson said that she agreed.

Exercise: Put the following example of direct speech into reported speech (and third person if necessary).

"We should progress this," he said.

....

....

"Be realistic – we can't afford it," she said.

....

....

"The plan has worked," she said.

....

....

"We've been having a very successful year," they said.

....

....

Relationship with the chair

The relationship with the chairperson has come up quite a bit already in the book. We've looked at sitting next to the chairperson to help him/her run the meeting and so you can hear the conversations properly. We have discussed having a pre-meeting with the chair so you understand issues to be raised in the meeting.

We now want to think about this relationship in depth. First of all I want you to think about your chairperson – what could they do that would really help you to carry out your role as minute taker? What do they already do that you find really helpful? Imagine there are no limits; imagine that perfect chairperson! Make this list as specific as possible as this is a start to your action plan. For example, rather than stating, "I would like my chairperson to communicate more", you should write, "I would like a meeting with my chairperson a couple of days before the meeting I am to minute." Also, think about not just during the meeting, but before and after the meeting, and on an ongoing basis.

Exercise: Imagine the perfect chairperson.
List things they could do to help you with your role as the minute taker.

....
....
....
....
....
....
....
....
....
....

OK, so we've got some ideas but, if you go to your chair and say, "I've read a book on minute taking and I have some great ideas of what you can do to make my life easier," it may be a lead balloon moment. So, let's now think about what we, as minute takers, can offer in return.

Exercise: What could you do as the minute taker before, during, after the meeting and on an ongoing basis, to make life easier for your chairperson?
Focus particularly on things you do to help yourself and how these might also help your chair.

That's a bit more balanced now; here are some of my thoughts which may also help if you haven't thought of them already:

What can the chairperson do to help the minute taker?

✓ Make time for a pre-meeting with the minute taker

✓ Include the minute taker in other pre-meetings taking place for the meeting they are to minute

✓ Give the minute taker plenty of notice that they are required to minute a meeting (so often meetings are arranged, a chairperson selected and then the minute taker is only decided as an afterthought at the last minute)

✓ Tell the minute taker how detailed minutes need to be

✓ Give the minute taker an idea of the sort of information required in the minutes

✓ Warn the minute taker of any particular issues to be aware of

✓ Support the minute taker by ensuring other people give any help required

✓ Run the meeting effectively keeping control of attendees and allowing only one person to speak at a time

✓ Introduce everyone if necessary, including the minute taker (although he or she may not be involved in the meeting, they are a vital part of the process and should not be ignored)

✓ Summarize main points and actions as the meeting progresses

✓ Ensure regular breaks are included in meetings over a couple of hours long – the minute taker has to concentrate for 100% of the time; nobody can do that for more than two hours

✓ Agree on what the minute taker should do if they haven't heard or understood something

✓ Respect the role of the minute taker

✓ Give the minute taker feedback on their minutes; explain why you have made changes to what they have written

✓ Explain their policy of recording Any Other Business

What can the minute taker do to help the chairperson?

✓ Prepare a draft agenda for the chairperson to save them time and also enable the minute taker to have more time to prepare

✓ Prepare documentation beforehand to ensure a smooth running meeting

✓ Attend pre-meetings to ensure proper preparation for the meeting

✓ Make sure all the logistics are in place (meeting room, refreshments, etc)

✓ Get informed about the subject matter
  • to reduce the amount of clarification and explanation required (particularly during a meeting)
  • and to make sure the minutes are written accurately and don't need to be corrected (which takes time)

✓ Produce a chairperson's agenda

✓ Mark documents with relevant agenda item number

✓ Clarify how much detail is needed in the minutes

✓ Get to know the meeting attendees

✓ Warn the chairperson of any issues which may arise

✓ Help the chair to run the meeting by keeping an eye on the time or having useful information to hand

✓ Develop the role of the minute taker to successfully support the chairperson

✓ Maintain a positive attitude

✓ Follow up actions (if appropriate)

✓ Respect the chairperson's role

✓ Ask for feedback on the minutes produced

As you can see, these ideas overlap; which is good. Basically, whatever helps the minute taker, helps the chairperson and vice versa.

If you want to encourage your chairperson to do some of these things, tell them why it is in their interests as well as yours.

Perhaps you could now produce a good practice document for your department outlining the roles of a good chairperson, minute taker and meeting attendee.

Assertiveness

It is impossible to be assertive if you are not confident. You are an important part of the meeting process and you must feel confident in your abilities. So, let us first have a look at how to be more confident.

How to be more confident:

- ✓ Develop a positive attitude – if you see life in a positive way, it will seem better and you will feel more confident; if you always expect the worse, you won't feel very confident.
- ✓ Concentrate on your strengths – we sometimes tend to focus on what we are bad at and the mistakes we have made. I agree with reflecting on our actions, but then you must decide how you will avoid this happening again. Then you must think about the things you have done well, your successes; this will make you feel more confident.
- ✓ Know your subject.
- ✓ Use confident body language – shoulders back, head high, making eye contact, open arms – you will automatically feel more confident and people will have confidence in you because you look confident – a virtuous circle.
- ✓ Think first – always give yourself time before you answer questions or give opinions.
- ✓ Don't have a negative attitude, concentrate on positive things
- ✓ Be proud of what you are – you are never 'just a secretary'.
- ✓ Confidence builds confidence.
- ✓ Take deep breaths.
- ✓ Plan your strategy – think about what you will say, do, wear, etc before going into difficult situations.
- ✓ Don't apologize – discuss. Often people have a habit of apologizing for things that are not their fault – try not to – sorry!
- ✓ Speak clearly and at the right time - don't feel you have to fill the gap (I'll explain this shortly).
- ✓ Think about something you know you are confident about and can do very well. It doesn't have to be anything to do with work at all, just something that you're sure you know how to do. Why do you feel confident in this situation?"
- ✓ Say you're not sure if you're not – it's OK not to know everything.

Exercise: Your body position can help your confidence levels. Have a go at the following.

First, bow your head, droop your shoulders, fold your arms tightly, look around the room furtively, think about something a bit sad (not very). Stay like that for a moment or two.

How did you feel?

....

....

....

....

Your physiology affects your mood and vice versa.

If you want to appear and feel confident, you need to sit up straight, head up, open your arms, shoulders back and look directly at something in the room. Think of something you enjoy doing and you are good at. It doesn't have to have anything at all to do with work.

Now how do you feel?

....

....

....

....

....

So if you don't really feel confident, act as if you are by changing your body position and thinking of something you're good at.

What is assertiveness?

It is the "happy medium" between being passive and aggressive. Passive people are afraid to say what they think and eventually can become very bitter and angry inside. Aggressive people don't care what anyone else thinks and are only interested in what they want; passive people irritate them and make them more aggressive. This causes the passive person to become even more passive.

An assertive person is not afraid to say what they think, but will always take into account other people's needs.

Why are assertiveness skills important for a minute taker?

➢ You may have to speak up in a meeting to ask questions or get clarification on a point.

➢ You need to ensure that you get the information you need from the chairperson or other meeting attendees.

➢ You may have to chase people to get papers for a meeting or to take actions afterwards.

➢ You want to convince people to help you get informed before the meeting.

➢ It will make you a more effective administrator.

Here are some ways to be more assertive:

➢ **Being confident (see the previous section)**

➢ **Knowledge**

You cannot be assertive if you don't understand the issues. Make sure you fully understand what the meeting is about when you are going to take minutes.

➢ **Voice control**

Being assertive is not just about saying the right words, you have to have the correct tone of voice to convince other people that you are assertive. Speak clearly and loudly enough and make sure your sentences don't just trail off.

➢ **State the facts**

➢ **Be honest**

➢ **No emotion or exaggeration**
Say what you think without being too emotional and without any exaggeration,"I've told you a million times not to do that" is very aggressive, and blatantly not true; rather say "I have mentioned this to you before."

➢ **Aim to achieve the best solution for all concerned**
Use the word 'we' rather than 'you'; this can sound more friendly and less accusing. ("We need to look at how the meeting is organized.")

➢ **Don't "fill the gap"**
We often come across as less assertive and more passive by continuing to speak ('waffling'). An assertive person will say what they have to say and then stop – not 'filling the gap'. Just let the other person speak; don't be embarrassed by silence...

➢ **Give yourself time**
We often feel we have to reply straightaway, but it is OK to give yourself time to think about your replies. Also, don't feel you have to keep talking or justifying your thoughts and decisions. Say what you have to say and then stop (as above).

➢ **Don't accuse**
"You made a mess of that" would be very aggressive; rather say "we need to talk about how this is done."

➢ **Avoid being passive or aggressive**

➢ **Ask questions**
If someone is trying to force you into a situation you are not happy with, turn things around and ask questions. For example, "What would you do in my situation?" or "Do you think that's a good idea?"

➢ **Body language**
Even more important than the words you use and your tone of voice is your body language. A person picking up signals from you will read most from your gestures and stance. Ensure you stand up straight, have your arms open and your head up to convince people that you are confident and assertive. Don't go too far and become aggressive!

> ➤ **Plan ahead**

ALWAYS think in advance about how you are going to deal with a situation; what you are going to say, how will you stand, how will you pitch your voice. Think about how you will introduce the topic, what will someone say back to you and what would you then say. What else might they say and how would you reply if they said that? What about if they say something you haven't thought about; what would you say/do then? All this will make you feel so much more confident.

So, how can we use this in meetings?

✓ Be confident by remembering that you are a vital part of the meeting system. You have an important role to play and you are an equal with your colleagues in this activity.

✓ Be confident by having prepared beforehand so you understand the discussion and the issues and you know what is important.

✓ Be confident by having had a meeting with the chairperson beforehand so you know what he/she requires of you and what information they would like you to record. You can also establish ground rules for things like interruptions, misunderstandings, timing, etc.

✓ Be confident by having a good working relationship with the chairperson and other attendees.

✓ Ensure you have as much information about the meeting, attendees and topics beforehand.

✓ If you need to ask questions during the meeting, ensure your voice is clear and controlled. Get people's attention before you ask your question. "Excuse me, could I just clarify the last point?" or "Excuse me, may I ask a question here?" Speak a little slower than usual and don't let your voice trail off. Stop when you have said what you want to say. Waving your arms around and saying, "Hang on, I didn't get that," may not get the reaction you would like!

✓ Ensure your body language is assertive; if you look submissive, aggressive people will glare at you and make you feel worse. Sit up straight, make eye contact and don't fiddle with pens or your hair.

✓ Plan ahead the sort of phrases you might use in various situations such as interrupting or being criticized. I had experience of being bullied in meetings and, at the time, had no idea how to deal with this. I felt embarrassed, upset and was then not able to take notes effectively. In fact, it wasn't until a few years later that I even realized it was bullying; I thought it was normal practice. Of course, if bullying is affecting your health and well-being you must take appropriate action.

Exercise: Are there any changes you need to make to the way you work with other people to help you perform your role better?

What to record

One of the most common worries that delegates on my courses have is that of knowing what information to write in the minutes. Clearly I cannot tell you exactly what you need to include in your minutes, but below are some things that should definitely be included:

Remember, just because you write it in your notes, doesn't mean it has to go in the minutes – if you are in doubt, write something in your notes and decide later whether or not to type it in the minutes.

✓ Date, time, location of meeting

✓ Attendees and apologies

✓ Details of next meeting

✓ Mention any papers tabled or discussed.
However, don't include a lot of information from a paper if there is no new information coming out of the discussion; just write 'see attached'.

✓ Proposals (motions) should be written verbatim.
This is in very formal meetings and you would most likely have the wording of the proposal beforehand anyway.

✓ Action points, who is responsible and a deadline (if one is cited). Actions need three facts: who, what and when.

✓ Decisions made (and the main arguments for and against). Include anything that changes any existing situation or issue. Discuss with the chairperson whether or not to include arguments; this will often depend on who is to read the minutes.

✓ Information that is required by people not at the meeting and on which they need to act.
Do you include more information for someone who was absent but who was given an action, or will the chairperson just speak to him/her privately?

✓ Information that should be kept on record.
For health & safety reasons, legal reasons, company policy reasons, etc; the chairperson should know what is needed and make sure you are also aware.

✓ Read previous minutes to see what has been recorded in the past and in how much detail.
If you think they are too detailed, be assertive and suggest summarizing is used more. People are overloaded with information nowadays and would, I'm sure, appreciate more succinct minutes to read.

✓ A space at the end for the Chairperson to sign and date.

Exercise: What do you have to record for your organization?

....
....
....
....
....
....
....
....
....
....
....

Exercise: Action plan - having thought about the skills a minute taker should have, what do you think you should do to improve your own skills? Make the actions easy to achieve by making them small and having a date on them.

....
....
....
....
....
....
....
....
....
....
....
....
....
....
....
....
....
....
....
....
....

Item 4:
Examples of Minutes

"I try to leave out the parts that people skip."
Elmore Leonard

Item 4:
Examples of Minutes

Objectives for item 4, at the end of this item you will:

✓ Have examples of different types of minutes

✓ Have designed a layout for your minutes

Layout of minutes:

Exercise: Get hold of some minutes from your company.
Is there a standard layout?
Are they easy to read?
Can you identify what the actions are and who should do them?
Can you match the minutes to the agenda for that same meeting?
How formal are they?
How are names used?

....
....
....
....
....
....

Checklist for laying out minutes

- ❑ Is the font clear to read?
  Advice from the dyslexia society says fonts should be straight (sans serif) like Arial or Calibri and at least 12 point.
  If it makes it easier for dyslexics to read it will help everyone else too.

- ❑ Is there plenty of space on the page?
  It is much easier for people to read text if there is not too much on each page.

- ❑ Are the agenda items in a different font/bold/capitals?
  It is important to be able to quickly pick out which agenda item the text belongs to.

- ❑ Are the agenda items in the same order in both the minutes and the original agenda?

- ❑ Is the use of names consistent throughout?

- ❑ Can actions be easily identified and do the minutes make it clear what the action is, who will be responsible and when it needs to be done by?

- ❑ Do you need a space for the chair to sign the minutes to say they are correct?

- ❑ Do you need to put your contact details on them?

- ❑ Is the date that the meeting took place on the minutes?

- ❑ Is the title of the meeting on the minutes?

Examples of minutes:

There are lots of examples of minutes on the internet. Here are a couple of different styles for you to look at. They are not necessarily perfect but they can give you ideas for different styles.

> Exercise: Have a look at the following minutes, what do you like about them? What could be improved?
>
> http://www.fsa.gov.uk/Pages/Library/corporate/Board/index.shtml
>
> http://www.south-norfolk.gov.uk/democracy/default.aspx?id=264.xml (brown ones with m on for minutes, reddish brown with a for agenda)
>
> http://www.council.bham.ac.uk/meetings/

Following are two examples for minuting meetings. The first is an example from an ad hoc meeting and the second from a more formal meeting with a full agenda.

From: The Manager
Sent: 29 July 20XX 12:16
To: All staff
Subject: NEW IT SYSTEM

Further to our meeting this morning, please find below a summary of the points we agreed.

1. **Information session**
    Clients will be informed of the changes in an email to be sent by Erin Smith.

2. **Training**
    Training will be held on 13 August and 14 August – 10 people to attend each session.

TEACHING COLLEGE MINUTES

Minutes of the Health and Safety Committee Meeting held in room G104 at 4pm on 9th July 20XX.

PRESENT

Erin Smith, Health & Safety Officer (Chairperson) (ES)

Ian Jones, Administration Officer (IJ)

Aarlif Hussain, Staff Welfare Co-ordinator (AH)

Bradley Pitt, Department Representative (BP)

George Coney, Estates Manager (GC)

IN ATTENDANCE

Jo Smith (Secretary) (JS)

1. APOLOGIES FOR ABSENCE   ACTION

Apologies were received from Brian Jones and Angela Green.

2. MINUTES OF PREVIOUS MEETING

The minutes of the previous meeting were taken as read, agreed as a true and correct record and signed by the Chairperson.

3. MATTERS ARISING

George Coney reported that the recent fire drills had been successful and all the issues raised last time had been resolved.

4. NEW BUILDING REGULATIONS

These were effective from 1 October 20XX. Members agreed that all staff must be informed of the implications.

A copy of the surveyor's letter was circulated and will be discussed in a meeting to be arranged for next week.

ES, 14/7/XX

5. PLANNED IT UPDATES

It was proposed that these would be undertaken by Ace Technology during October and November to minimize disruption to operations. George Coney will meet with Ace next week to discuss plans.

GC, 15/7/XX

6. ANY OTHER BUSINESS

Aarlif Hussain raised the issue of bank holidays and has asked members to give him their thoughts at the next meeting.

All

7. DATE AND TIME OF NEXT MEETING

It was agreed that the next meeting should be held at 4pm on 10 October 20XX.

Signed .... (Chairperson)   Date....................

Item 5:
Minute Writing Exercise

"It's not necessarily the amount of time you spend at practice that counts; it's what you put into the practice." Eric Lindros

Item 5:
Minute Writing Exercise

Objectives for item 5, at the end of this item you will:

✓ Have practiced your new skills by writing minutes from a script

Exercise: Use the transcript below to write a set of minutes for the meeting. You can assume that everyone, that was there, spoke at least once.

AGENDA for the staff meeting on Weds 4th April

1. Apologies

2. Minutes of the previous meeting

3. Matters arising

4. Staff canteen accounts

5. Reception refurbishment

6. Student placements

7. Summer barbecue

8. Any other business

9. Date of next meeting

Meeting transcript

Lily Green (Chairperson)	Good afternoon everyone. Taylor Black won't be here today; he's had to meet up with our contacts at Colors Limited.
	Was everyone happy with the last minutes?
	(all nod)
	Can we sign them?
	(Chairperson signs)
	Good, matters arising? Anything to report?
Bradley Brown	Daisy and I spoke to Heather about her training and we've agreed to finance this. She won't be here for the next meeting as she will be on the first day.
Chairperson	That's good. Right, let's move on to item 4. Marcus, you wanted to discuss the accounts for the canteen. Can we see copies of these?
Marcus Blue	Yes, I have copies for everyone (distributes copies). We made a profit of £1,300 over the first 6 months of the year. I thought it would be a good idea to get some new chairs with some of the money – the existing ones are a bit wobbly!
Chairperson	Good idea, Marcus, but could you get some costs for us at look at during the next meeting?
	(Mr Blue agrees)

Chairperson	OK let's look at the next item. Some people have commented that our reception area is looking rather tatty.
Hazel Fawn	I thought the same, it needs redecorating and modernizing.
Chairperson	Who would like to get some quotes for this?
Hazel Fawn	Yes, I'll do that. We've got some good contacts we can speak to.
Chairperson	Right, that's something else to continue with next time. Cameron, you're next.
Cameron White	We would like to start taking on work experience students, which will hopefully raise the company's profile and give us access to new staff as we expand.
	We could perhaps take on two students in September and pay them if possible.
Hazel Fawn	That would be an excellent idea.
Chairperson	I agree, but I don't think we can authorize it. Cameron, would you email the directors and ask them to discuss it at the board meeting and let us know their decision?
Cameron White	I will.

Chairperson	Now, the final item. Summer barbeque. Rose, have you got the menus?
Rose Pink	Yes, I was able to get hold of quite a few. (distributes copies)
Cameron White	I like the look of the Canalside Hotel menu and they have facilities for if it rains.
Bradley Brown	It does look good – not too expensive either.
Rose Pink	Shall we go for that one then? (agreement)
Chairperson	What date seems the best?
Rose Pink	The last Friday evening in June will work for the majority of staff?
Chairperson	That's great, Rose, can you make the arrangements?
Rose Pink	Yes, I'll book the hotel and send an email to all the staff. Should be good.
Chairperson	I'm looking forward to it. Any other business, anyone? No? OK, let's meet again in 3 weeks' time.

Example answer:

Minutes of the staff meeting held on Weds 4th April

Present:
Lily Green (chair), Marcus Blue, Bradley Brown, Hazel Fawn, Rose Pink, Cameron White, Glenda Green (Minutes)

1   Apologies

Apologies were received from Taylor Black

2   Minutes of the previous meeting

The minutes of the previous meeting were taken as read, agreed as a true and correct record and signed by the Chairperson.

3   Matters arising

Bradley Brown and Daisy had agreed to finance Heather's training, which starts on 25th April.

4   Staff canteen accounts

Marcus Blue distributed copies of the canteen accounts which showed a profit of £1,300 over the first 6 months of the year.

It was suggested that new chairs be bought with some of this profit and Marcus agreed to obtain estimates for discussion at the next meeting.

MB, 25/4

5   **Reception refurbishment**

Following comments that the reception area looked rather shabby, Hazel Fawn offered to get quotations for redecorating and modernizing. These will be discussed at the next meeting.

HF, 25/4

6   **Student placements**

Cameron White outlined proposals to take on work experience students to raise the company's profile and give access to new staff. He suggested two paid positions.

This was thought to be an excellent idea but the Chairperson stated that Board approval was required.

Cameron agreed to email the directors to ask them to discuss this at their meeting.

CW

7   **Summer barbeque**

Rose Pink agreed to book the Canalside Hotel   RP
for this event on 30 June and to send an email to inform all staff.

8   **Any other business**

There was no other business.

9   **Date of next meeting**

Weds 25th April

Notes:

....

....

....

....

....

....

....

....

....

....

....

....

....

....

....

....

....

....

....

Item 6:
Checklist and Action Plan

*"Great things are done by a series of
small things brought together."*
Vincent van Gogh

Item 6:
Checklist and
Action Plan

Objectives for item 6, at the end of this item you will:

✓ Have looked at the checklist of tasks and tailored it to fit your timings

✓ Have produced an action plan to ensure you put into practice your new skills

On the next couple of pages is a checklist to help you with your role as a minute taker. The timings are based on a small meeting that doesn't take place too often (for example a monthly project meeting). For each meeting you're involved with you need to talk to the chair to find out which parts of the checklist you will be responsible for and what your actual timings should be.

Checklist for successful meeting organization

The suggested timings work for most meetings but this will depend on the nature of your business and how well your systems work so you need to fill in your actual timings.

Before the meeting:

	Details	Suggested timing before	Your timing
1	Arrange meeting with all attendees	3-4 weeks	
2	Book room, refreshments and equipment (be aware of any special needs)	3-4 weeks	
3	Nominate chairperson and minute taker	3-4 weeks	
4	Draft agenda	2 weeks	
5	Get informed on topics to be discussed	2 weeks	
6	Speak to or meet any attendees who can increase your knowledge	2 weeks	
7	Meet with the chairperson to discuss requirements for the meeting and the minutes and agree agenda	1 week	
8	Distribute agenda and papers	1 week	
9	Email to remind people to bring papers from the previous meeting, such as minutes	1 week	
10	Start writing your minutes on the template now saved as a word document	1 week	
11	Prepare your dress and behavior (what shall I wear, what might I say)	1 week	
12	Check refreshments are OK	2 days	
13	Seating plan, if required	2 days	
14	Ensure you have plenty of paper and pens (or a laptop – is there plenty of battery time left?)	1 day	
15	Arrive at the meeting room early to set up and check – select your and the chairperson's seats if not already assigned	On the day	
16	Greet people as they arrive. Unless it is specifically part of your role, don't get involved in making/ serving drinks as this is a distraction from minute taking. If it is your role, you may want to question this.	On the day	

During the meeting:

	Details
1	Keep an eye on the time for the chairperson; timings can be included on the agenda
2	Listen
3	Take notes, not minutes
4	Interact assertively when required
5	Assist the chairperson as agreed

After the meeting:

	Details	Suggested timing after	Your timing
1	Review your notes as quickly as possible	On the day	
2	Start typing the minutes – just a rough draft first of all	On the day or 1 day later	
3	Summarize the meeting and convert your notes to minutes	Next 2-3 days	
4	Proofread your minutes	Day after writing minutes	
5	Ask the chairperson to check the minutes if necessary	Next 3-4 days	
6	Distribute as appropriate	As soon as ready	
7	Go back to beginning of this list for the next meeting!		

Personal action plan

What was I most worried about regarding minute taking?
How am I going to deal with this?

....

....

....

....

....

Five things I am going to do from the next working day to
improve my minute taking skills:

....

....

....

....

....

Five things I am going to do from the following week to improve my minute taking skills:

....

....

....

....

....

Further training I would like to pursue:

....

....

....

....

....

....

....

....

....

....

....

....

Final farewell

At the beginning of this book I wrote about how frightened I used to be when taking minutes and how I was aware many people feel exactly the same way.

Often it is easy to fall back on the 'we've always done it like this' route and minutes are produced which are full of business clichés, ridiculously wordy and like something from the 1950s. We need to move into the 21st century and produce brief, clear and effective minutes that enable people to become informed quickly and accurately.

I hope the information in this book has addressed the issues you had with taking notes and writing minutes and that you will now take action to become a truly effective minute taker.

I would love to hear about your experiences and any comments on the book (support@UoLearn.com) – we can hopefully introduce them into the next update!

Notes:

....

....

....

....

....

....

....

....

....

....

....

....

....

....

....

....

....

....

....

....

....

....

Item 7:
Answers to Exercises

"Dreams are today's answers to tomorrow's questions."
Edgar Cayce

Item 7:
Answers to some
of the exercises

Page 48

<u>Verbs</u>, underlined, **nouns** bold and adjectives grey.

1. The usual **chairperson** <u>read</u> the **minutes**.

2. It <u>was agreed</u> to <u>increase</u> the annual **salaries**.

3. **Mr Smith** <u>volunteered</u> to <u>send</u> an explanatory **email**.

4. **KL** <u>said</u> that **he** <u>would try out</u> the new **system**.

Page 50

1. He had been **practicing(US) practising(UK)** medicine for years.

2. It was a nice **compliment** about my work.

3. The **principal** reason why the project succeeded was the team management.

4. The chairperson was concerned about the **effect** this would have on the **practice** time.

Page 55

1. The clients' rooms are nearby.

2. The manager's response was "no".

3. The secretaries' attitude must improve.

4. The men's preference was to sit down.

5. The caretaker says that he's happy with this plan.

6. You're not sure what your choice will be.

7. It's difficult to know if the company and its representatives are included.

8. The SATs were very difficult.

Page 57

It was agreed that the manager would probably outline her plans to the department. The chairperson reported the CEO's comment that everyone should be told of the likelihood of redundancies. She added that she concurred with this.

Page 66

1. Based on the improved sales figures, it was agreed that a bonus could be paid this year.

2. Mr Jones agreed to contact the Board to obtain permission to carry out required repairs to the new offices.

3. The proposed new pay system will be implemented.

4. It was noted that a profit of £13 million had been made in the 6 months to 30th June.

1. **Apologies for absence**
No apologies were received.

2. **Minutes of the last meeting**
The Chairperson asked members to correct an error in item 3.1, where the figure of £11,200 should read £111,200. After this amendment, the minutes were approved and signed by the Chairperson as a correct record.

3. **Matters arising**
There were no matters arising.

4. **Chairperson's report**
The Chairperson pointed out that over the last 6 months membership had fallen by 20%. She felt that this was due largely to lack of publicity during the present year, and also that new employees were not aware of how to join. The following decisions were reached.
4.1   Circular to all staff
A letter would be sent from the Chairperson to all employees who were not members of the Club. This letter would outline its aims and activities. A tear-off slip would be included for employees to indicate any areas of interest.   CW
4.2   Social evening
A social evening would be organized specifically for non-members, to include refreshments. Miss Chen agreed to make the arrangements.   CC

5. **New aerobics classes**
Miss Carol Chen proposed that aerobics classes should be held. Mrs Sharon Warner from the Cool Gym had agreed to conduct these classes on the Company's premises every Wednesday evening from 6-7pm.
Miss Chen will provide further information.   CC

6. **Any other business**
There was no other business.

Page 71

1. He said this should be progressed.

2. She stated that realistically it could not be afforded.

3. She said the plan had worked.

4. They said they had been having a very successful year.

Item 8:
Index

"Order and simplification are the first steps toward the mastery of a subject." Thomas Mann

Index

Item 9:
Universe of Learning Books

"The purpose of learning is growth, and our minds, unlike our bodies, can continue growing as we continue to live." Mortimer Adler

About the publishers

Universe of Learning Limited is a small publisher based in the UK with production in England, Australia and America. Our authors are all experienced trainers or teachers who have taught their skills for many years. We are actively seeking qualified authors and if you visit the authors section on www.UoLearn.com you can find out how to apply.

If you are interested in any of our current authors (including Heather Baker) coming to speak at your event please do visit their own websites (for Heather it's www.bakerthompsonassoc. co.uk) or email them through the author section of the UoLearn site.

If you would like to purchase larger numbers of books then please do contact us (sales@UoLearn.com). We give discounts from 5 books upwards. For larger volumes we can also quote for changes to the cover to accommodate your company logo and to the interior to brand it for your company.

All our books are written by teachers, trainers or people well experienced in their roles and our goal is to help people develop their skills with a well structured range of exercises.

If you have any feedback about this book or other topics that you'd like to see us cover please do contact us at support@UoLearn.com.

Keep Learning!

Speed Writing

Speedwriting for faster
note taking and dictation

ISBN 978-1-84937-011-0 from www.UoLearn.com

Easy exercises to learn faster writing in just 6 hours.

✓ "The principles are very easy to follow, and I am already using it to take notes."
✓ "I will use this system all the time."
✓ "Your system is so easy to learn and use."

Report Writing

An easy to follow format
for writing business reports

ISBN 978-1-84937-036-3, from www.UoLearn.com

This book makes report writing a step by step process for you to follow every time you have a report to write.

✓ How to set objectives using 8 simple questions
✓ Easy to follow flow chart
✓ How to write an executive summary
✓ How to layout and structure the report
✓ Help people remember what they read

Successful Business Writing

How to write excellent
and persuasive communications

ISBN 978-1-84937-074-5, from www.uolearn.com

✓ Think about the purpose of the communication
✓ Create successful text for emails, letters, minutes, reports, brochures, websites, and social media
✓ Write effective communications to persuade people
✓ Sample letters and emails
✓ Know how to write good English

Coaching Skills Training Course

Business and life coaching techniques for

ISBN: 978-1-84937-019-6, from www.uolearn.com
- ✓ An easy to follow 5 step model
- ✓ Learn to both self-coach and coach others
- ✓ Over 25 ready to use ideas
- ✓ Goal setting tools to help achieve ambitions

A toolbox of ideas to help you become a great coach.

Stress Management

Exercises and techniques to manage stress and anxiety

ISBN: 978-1-84937-002-8, from www.uolearn.com
- ✓ Understand what stress is
- ✓ Become proactive in managing your stress
- ✓ How to become more positive about your life
- ✓ An easy 4 step model to lasting change

Practical and Effective Performance Management

ISBN: 978-1-84937-037-0, from www.uolearn.com
- ✓ Five key ideas to understanding performance
- ✓ A clear four step model
- ✓ Key what works research that is practical
- ✓ A large, wide ranging choice of tools
- ✓ Practical exercises and action planning for managers

A toolbox of ideas to help you become a better leader.

Developing Your Influencing Skills

ISBN: 978-1-84937-004-2, from www.uolearn.com
- ✓ Decide what your influencing goals are
- ✓ Find ways to increase your credibility rating
- ✓ Develop stronger and more trusting relationships
- ✓ Inspire others to follow your lead
- ✓ Become a more influential communicator

Packed with case studies, exercises and practical tips to become more influential.

Studying for your Future

Skills for life, whilst you study

ISBN: 978-1-84937-047-9, Order at www.uolearn.com

✓ A checklist to put together a portfolio to show a prospective employer
✓ Learn the skills to prepare you for your degree
✓ Help you with literature reviews and writing skills
✓ Goal setting to help you focus on your future
✓ Sort out your time planning
✓ Improve your study skills and exam preparation
✓ Prepare for employment

How to Start a Business as a Private Tutor

ISBN 978-1-84937-029-5, from www.uolearn.com

This book, by a Lancashire based author, shows you how to set up your own business as a tutor.

✓ Packed with tips and stories
✓ How to get started - what to do and buy
✓ How to attract clients and advertise
✓ Free printable forms, ready to use
✓ Advice on preparing students for exams

Dreaming Yourself Aware

Exercises to interpret your dreams

ISBN: 978-1-84937-055-4, Order at www.uolearn.com

✓ Learn how to remember and record your dreams
✓ Structured approach to understand your dreams
✓ A large variety of techniques for dream interpretation
✓ Step by step instructions and worked examples
✓ Exercises to help you to find answers to problems
✓ Understand your motivation and reveal your goals
✓ Make positive changes to your life

Dreaming yourself aware gives a step by step guide to interpreting your dreams.

"A sentence should contain no unnecessary words,
a paragraph no unnecessary sentences,
for the same reason that a drawing should have no
unnecessary lines and a machine no unnecessary parts."
William Strunk, The Elements of Style

Lightning Source UK Ltd.
Milton Keynes UK
UKOW07f1823241116

288482UK00018B/527/P

9 781849 370769